English Reading Comprehension

Success in
Year 2

Written and illustrated
by Jim Edmiston

Acknowledgements:

Author: Jim Edmiston
Cover and Page Design: Jim Edmiston and Kathryn
Webster

The right of Jim Edmiston to be identified as the author of this publication
has been asserted by him in accordance with the Copyright, Designs and
Patents Act 1988.

HeadStart Primary Ltd
Elker Lane
Clitheroe
BB7 9HZ

T. 01200 423405
E. info@headstartprimary.com
www.headstartprimary.com

Published by HeadStart Primary Ltd © **HeadStart Primary Ltd**

A record for this book is available from the British Library -
ISBN: 978-1-908767-33-2

HeadStart

primary

Year 2

CONTENTS

Test Administration Guidance

SCALED SCORE TEST A Can't
Do Anything
The Rubbish Band

SCALED SCORE TEST B
The Slow-worm
The Night Patrol
Nocturnal Animals
A Lovely Day for a Picnic

SCALED SCORE TEST C
Seeing Rainbows
The Emperor Who Hated Yellow (Part 1)
The Emperor Who Hated Yellow (Part 2)

Answers, Mark Schemes and Progress Tracking/Scaled Score Information

V3

INTRODUCTION

HeadStart Primary English Reading Comprehension has been produced to make the teacher's formative assessment of reading as straightforward as possible. At the same time, its aim is to develop children's reading skills and encourage their engagement with literature in all its forms.

With this in mind, sections have been organised to follow closely the national curriculum and the different reading skills (content domains) highlighted in the KS1 English Reading Test Framework 2016 (available to download at www.gov.uk), with an emphasis, at this key stage, on the **comprehension** aspects of the curriculum.

The tasks presented here increase in difficulty as you work through a section. This allows for:

- easier access for the child still acquiring and developing basic skills

- a challenge for the child whose skills are more secure

- a further challenge and consolidation for the child who is in the process of exceeding year group expectations.

This structure enables the teacher to monitor the progress a child is making in each particular skill area and, as a result, will ease the process of formative assessment. An individual child, for instance, may have a wide vocabulary but lack inferential skills. The organisation of tasks will make this apparent so that the child's learning can be moved forward.

A range of fiction and non-fiction underpins the reading tasks as well as the range of texts in the **TESTS** section. Since the removal of national curriculum levels, schools are now free to choose their own methods of monitoring progress in reading. The tests here have been provided to help the process of formative assessment, but they could be used simply as further practice tasks or to allow children to glimpse a test format. This is for the professional judgement of the class teacher.

An important reminder: the content of statutory tests does not include every element of the national curriculum, which should still be used for planning purposes and breadth of study.

Finally, the texts have been chosen in relation to Year 2 subject areas, their age-appropriate spelling lists and with the enjoyment of reading in mind.

Words in context

WHAT'S MISSING?

These sentences have a word missing. Choose the right word from the box and write it in the space.

city	runner	middle
fudge	apple	jacket
bottle	Everybody	table

1.   The _____ my Grandma makes is very sweet.

2.   The sleeve of my _____ was inside-out.

3.   Before going for a walk, I filled my _____ with water.

4.   Our cat is not allowed to jump onto the _____.

5.   _____ clapped when Ravi sang a song.

6.   I had a cheese sandwich and an _____ for lunch.

7.   The _____ is full of cars and busy people.

8.   Myra is the fastest _____ in our class.

9.   In the _____ of the night, I heard an owl.

MY GRANDAD THE GARDENER

Read this text about gardening, then answer the questions about what some of the words mean.

My Grandad the Gardener

My grandad just loves gardening. Every day, you will find him digging or planting seeds. When I visit him, he is always very cheerful. As soon as I step into the garden, he hands me a trowel and shows me where to begin weeding. Now, it's something I like to do as well. The scent of the flowers and the buzzing of the bees on a sunny day – these are all part of a wonderful day with Grandad in the garden.

1.   What word tells you Grandad enjoys gardening very much?

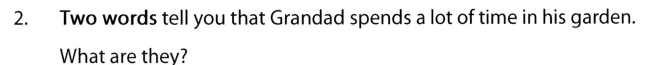

   _____

2.   **Two words** tell you that Grandad spends a lot of time in his garden. What are they?

   _____

3.   What word means **putting seeds in the ground**?

   _____

4. Copy down a word that means **going to see somebody in their home.**

_____

5. What word tells you that Grandad is happy?

_____

6. A small tool used for digging and weeding is mentioned. What is it?

_____

7. Find and write down another word that means **start.**

_____

8. What word tells you that the flowers have a sweet smell?

_____

9. What word is used to tell you what sound the bees make?

_____

10. What word tells you that spending a day in the garden is great?

_____

A MIX-UP AT THE ZOO

Daisy has just had her first day working at the zoo. This is her letter to her grandmother, but she's put the names of the animals in the wrong places.

Dear Gran,

The zoo was great. The **camel** spent a long time swinging in

its tree. The **dolphin** made a lot of noise, hee-hawing, but I didn't

mind. The **donkey** swam happily in its pool. The **giraffe**,

with its two humps, gave the children rides. The **monkey**,

with its long neck was able to reach the leaves high up in the trees.

Lots of love,

Daisy

Can you sort out her letter, putting the animals in the right places?

Dear Gran,

The zoo was great. The _____ spent a long time swinging in

its tree. The _____ made a lot of noise, hee-hawing, but I didn't

mind. The _____ swam happily in its pool. The _____,

with its two humps, gave the children rides. The _____,

with its long neck was able to reach the leaves high up in the trees.

Lots of love,

Daisy

WHAT'S MISSING?

Look at these sentences. They have a word missing. **Tick** the word that is missing from the sentence.

1.   In the forest, I saw a _____ digging a hole.

     badger ☐   **badge** ☐

2.   Dad gave me a _____ when I won the race.

     huge ☐   **hug** ☐

3.   I was scared when the rhino started to _____ .

     charge ☐   **change** ☐

4.   My mother asked me to _____ a thank-you note to Gran.

     right ☐   **write** ☐

5.   The astronaut was given a _____ when he returned to Earth.

     medal ☐   **metal** ☐

6.   We covered the tree with _____ at Christmas.

     tonsil ☐   **tinsel** ☐

7. The _____ climbed to the top of the tree.

donkey ☐   monkey ☐

8. In the desert, animals have to _____ with the heat.

cope ☐   copy ☐

9. I had to _____ after digging in the garden.

wash ☐   watch ☐

10. The story I'm reading has some very long _____ in it.

worlds ☐   words ☐

11. The robin ate a _____ for breakfast.

worm ☐   warm ☐

12. I couldn't get to sleep for the noise of the _____.

wild ☐   wind ☐

13. The _____ of some birds are quite long.

breaks ☐   beaks ☐

THE GREEN BLOBBY MONSTER

Here is a story with missing words. All
of the words are being held up by the
Green Blobby Monster. See if you can
put the right words in the right places.

snoring   bear
breath   pencils
biscuit   comb
pie   sleep   box

The Green Blobby Monster

Zuzu has lost something. It isn't her favourite, snuggly blanket. It

isn't her cuddly teddy _____. And it isn't the _____

she uses to do her squiggly hair. She's lost her Green Blobby Monster.

It's time for bed. But Zuzu can't _____. She won't be

happy until she's found her Green Blobby Monster.

She looks inside her toy _____. He's not hiding among the

cuddly elephants and giraffes.

Zuzu peers under the sofa. There's nothing there but a tiny

wind-up robot, a chocolate _____, a book full of blobby

things to colour in and some colouring _____.

She opens the fridge and peers inside. There's orange juice and a

cheese sandwich, but no Green Blobby Monster. The apple _____

has been eaten.

She runs all over the house until she's out of _____.

Now it's bed time. She looks under her bed. There is the Green Blobby

Monster, fast asleep and making a _____ noise.

It goes: "Zu...zu...zu...zu...zu..."

10

THE GIANT CALLED BOB

Read this story about a giant, then answer the questions that follow.

There was once a huge giant who lived at the edge of a beautiful village called Littletown. For a giant, Bob was very friendly. This was because he loved the jar of honey that Katie and Sam took him every day.

It wasn't a small jar. They had to shove it along the winding road on a cart. Then they had to get it across the river by the swinging bridge to where Bob lay in the shade of the trees.

One day, Katie and Sam arrived at the riverbank and noticed that a beaver had gnawed part of the bridge. They couldn't cross. They began to worry that Bob would get angry without his honey to keep him sweet.

Suddenly, it grew very gloomy. It was Bob's shadow. He wasn't angry. He smiled. He lifted up a tree trunk and placed it across the river. So then the villagers had a new bridge and Bob had his honey.

Search the story again to find words that mean the same as those in this list. Fill in the boxes.

meaning	word
very big	
very pretty	
liked very much	
little	
push	
nibbled	
twisty	
swaying	
saw	
came to	
very cross	
dark	

SOUNDS THE SAME – LOOKS DIFFERENT

The words in the boxes sound the same, but they mean different things.

Choose the right word for each sentence. **Fill in the gaps.**

be	OR	bee

1. What can it _____ like being a tiny insect?

2. I heard a _____ buzzing inside a flower.

been	OR	bean

3. You can't grow a beanstalk without a _____.

4. Have you _____ visiting the planet Mars?

see	OR	sea

5. We'll _____ if the tide is out when we get to the beach.

6. When we were swimming on holiday, the _____ was warm.

one	OR	won

7. _____ day, an Olympic runner came to our school.

8. A pupil from our school _____ a medal and was on television.

son	OR	sun

9.   Our teacher has a _____ who is in our class.

10.   When the _____ rises, it shines in my window.

blue	OR	blew

11.   I _____ out all the candles on my birthday cake.

12.   My favourite colour is _____.

hole	OR	whole

13.   Goldilocks saw the porridge and ate the _____ lot.

14.   I lost my money because I had a _____ in my pocket.

night	OR	knight

15.   Bats fly around our garden at _____.

16.   The _____ fought hard to rescue the princess.

Retrieving and recording information

Strand: Comprehension: identify / explain key aspects of fiction and non-fiction texts, such as characters, events, titles and information

National Curriculum reference:

- answering and asking questions
- explain and discuss their understanding of books, poems and other material, both those that they listen to and those that they read for themselves
- retrieving and recording information

Reading Test / Content Domain links: 1b

DOES CHOCOLATE GROW ON TREES?

Here is some information about chocolate. Read it carefully, then look at the sentences below. Decide if they are **true** or **false** and **tick the box**.

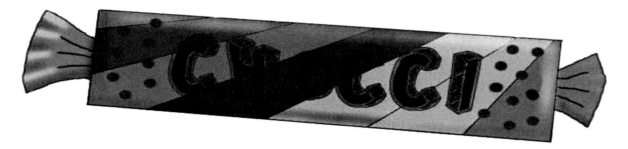

CHOCOLATE

Where does chocolate come from? Maybe you buy it in the supermarket or a local shop, but that's not where it starts.

First, you need a hot, wet place near the equator, such as parts of Africa and South America. There, you can grow cacao trees.

Each tree can have around 2000 rugby ball-shaped pods. Inside each pod there are lots of sticky beans, which have to be left to dry out. Sometimes they are roasted.

These are then taken to the factory to be ground down into powder ready to make chocolate. The factory could be across a vast ocean – nowhere near the cacao trees.

At last, it is delivered to your shop.

1. Cacao trees grow near the equator.   **TRUE** ☐   **FALSE** ☐

2. Cacao trees grow in Britain.   **TRUE** ☐   **FALSE** ☐

3. Each tree can grow 2000 beans.   **TRUE** ☐   **FALSE** ☐

4. Each pod contains one bean.   **TRUE** ☐   **FALSE** ☐

5. The beans are sticky.   **TRUE** ☐   **FALSE** ☐

6. The beans have to be boiled.   **TRUE** ☐   **FALSE** ☐

7. Sometimes the beans are roasted.   **TRUE** ☐   **FALSE** ☐

8. The factory can be miles away.   **TRUE** ☐   **FALSE** ☐

THE GREAT FIRE OF LONDON

A newspaper at the time of this event reported what happened.

The Gazette

September 1666

On the 2nd September, at one o' clock in the morning, there broke out a dreadful fire in the street known as Pudding Lane.

In that part of the town, the houses are built of timber. They are also so close to each other that it was easy for the fire to spread rapidly.

Panic followed, with the result that very little was done to prevent the march of the flames in every direction.

A few people did what they could by pulling down houses in its path. By the 6th September, the flames had died down.

---

1. Write down the time and date that the fire started?

    _____

    _____

2. What **two** reasons are given for the fire spreading so quickly?

    _____

    _____

3. How did some people try to stop the fire spreading?

    _____

ASTRONAUT: HELEN SHARMAN

Here is some information about British astronaut, Helen Sharman.

On 30th May, 1963, Helen Sharman was born in Sheffield.

She grew up very interested in science.

Then, one day, listening to the radio, she heard about a competition to pick someone to be an astronaut.

Lots of people – nearly 13,000 – asked to be part of this exciting competition. It was going to be on television.

On 25th November, 1989, Helen won. She was chosen to be the first British astronaut. Helen was the winner because of her skills as a scientist. After that, she had 18 months hard training in Star City in Russia. She had to learn Russian.

On 18th May, 1991, she was launched into space. Most of her eight days in space were spent working in the Mir Space Station.

While she was in space she:

- took photos of the British Isles

- chatted to schoolchildren over the radio

- did experiments with seeds to see how well they grew in space compared to Earth

FUN FACT:
At the time she was chosen, Helen was working for the company that makes Mars bars. Newspaper reporters wrote headlines such as:

Girl from Mars Blasts off to the Stars!

1.	When was Helen Sharman born?

   _____

2.	What happened on 25th November, 1989?

   _____

3.	How many people did she beat to become the winner?

   _____

4.	How did she know about the competition?

   _____

5.	How long did she have to train?

   _____

6.	At the time of the competition, who was she working for?

   _____

7.	How long was she in space?

   _____

8.	Write down **two** things she did while she was in space.

   _____

   _____

ASTRONAUT: TIM PEAKE

Here is some information about British astronaut, Tim Peake.

On 7th April, 1972, Tim Peake was born in Chichester.

In 1994, he became a helicopter pilot. Later, he beat over 8000 other people hoping to be trained to be astronauts.

Part of his training was to live under water for 12 days. He also had to learn to speak Russian so that he could talk to the other astronauts.

On 15th December 2015, he was launched into space with five other astronauts. They were heading for the International Space Station that orbits the Earth.

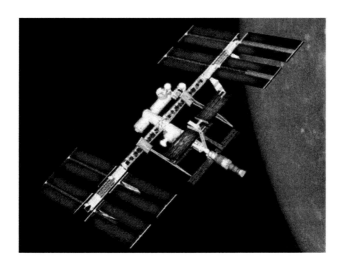

His first meal on the Space Station was a bacon sandwich and a cup of tea.

While orbiting the Earth, he gave science lessons to thousands of schoolchildren. He showed what zero gravity was like by doing back flips and playing ping pong with a bubble of water. On 15th January 2016, he became the first British astronaut to take part in a spacewalk outside the Space Station.

1. Where was Tim Peake born?

   _____

2. What did he start doing in 1994?

   _____

3. Write down one thing that was part of his training as an astronaut.

   _____

   _____

4. On 15th December 2015, how many astronauts were launched into space?

   _____

5. Where is the International Space Station?

   _____

6. What was Tim Peake's first meal on the Space Station?

   _____

7. He is the first British astronaut to have done something special. What is it?

   _____

   _____

THE GREAT BARRIER REEF

Here is some information about the biggest coral reef in the world.

FACT FILE

The Great Barrier Reef is the biggest coral reef in the world. It is over 1400 miles long.

Astronauts are able to see it from space.

The reef is off the north-east coast of Australia in the Coral Sea.

Coral reefs are built by millions of tiny creatures called polyps.

Polyps don't have a skeleton inside. Instead, they create a kind of skeleton on the outside. It's a hard, stony layer that protects them.

When the old polyps die, the stony layers are left. New polyps build hard layers on top of them, century after century.

This is how it builds up to a reef.

LIFE FORMS

Hundreds of different types of fish live along the reef. Angelfish, Parrotfish and Clownfish are a few colourful examples.

The shape of the coral helps to keep them safe from predators, but, of course, there are predators too.

The reef is also a habitat for sea horses, turtles, stingrays, sea snakes and sharks as well as whales and dolphins.

The Green Sea Turtle is one of the oldest reptiles, but it is in great danger. Some get caught in fishing nets; some are hunted for their shells.

The reef itself is under threat from climate change. Corals die when the sea is too warm for them. Pollution is making seas around the world warmer.

1. Where is the Great Barrier Reef?

   _____

2. **Two** facts tell us how big it is. Write down those **two** facts.

   _____

   _____

3. What is the name of the tiny creatures that create coral?

   _____

4. What are the names of the colourful fish that are mentioned?

   _____

   _____

   _____

5. Write down **two** things that are putting the Green Sea Turtle in danger.

   _____

   _____

6. How does pollution affect the coral reef?

   _____

   _____

A FABLE: THE MAN, THE BOY AND THE DONKEY

Read this fable (a story containing a lesson), then answer the questions.

The Man, the Boy, and the Donkey

A man and his son were taking their donkey to market. As they walked along by its side, a countryman passed and said, "You fools, what is a donkey for but to ride upon?" So the man put the boy on the donkey, and they went on their way.

Soon, they passed a group of men. One said, "See that lazy boy. He lets his father walk while he rides."

The man took his son off and climbed on himself. They hadn't gone far when they passed two women. One said to the other, "Shame on that lazy lout to let his poor son trudge along."

The man didn't know what to do, so he pulled his son up beside him on the donkey. When they reached the town, the people laughed and pointed at them. The man asked what they were laughing at.

The people said, "Aren't you ashamed of yourself for overloading that poor donkey of yours – you and your son?"

So they both got off and wondered what to do. They cut down a pole and tied the donkey's feet to it. Then they raised the pole and the donkey to their shoulders. They staggered along until they came to a bridge. The donkey, getting one of its feet loose, kicked out and caused the boy to drop his end of the pole. In the struggle the donkey fell over the bridge, and was drowned.

The old man and his son, feeling sad, made their way home, thinking: "When we try to please everybody, we please nobody."

Now check the fable again for the answers to these questions.

1. Who called the man and his son **fools**?

   _____

2. Who was the first one to sit on the donkey?

   _____

3. What word did the group of men use to describe the boy?

   _____

4. Who did the man and his son see after the group of men?

   _____

5. Where were they when people laughed and pointed at them?

   _____

6. What word tells you the man and his son found it hard to carry the donkey?

   _____

7. What happened to the donkey at the end?

   _____

8. What lesson did the man and his son learn?

   _____

MY FUNNY FAMILY

Here is a poem. You might like to perform it to the class. Answer the
questions after you've read it.

verse 1

Standing on stilts, my brother, Bradley,

Fell over backwards and hurt himself badly.

The doctors stood around, and whispered in a huddle,

"It could have been worse if he'd fallen in a puddle."

verse 2

My sister, Jane, is a terrible child.

She behaves like a tiger out in the wild.

She frightened the life out of our Aunt Mabel,

Growling and howling under the table.

verse 3

My cousin has a friend whose name is Kitty,

Who paints her face green and thinks she's pretty.

When she came on Sunday to play hide-and-seek,

She lay on the grass and stayed hidden for a week.

verse 4

There's nobody quite like old Uncle Norm,

Who went for a stroll in a thunderstorm.

He didn't wear a coat or a hat or a boot,

But splashed in the rain in his bathing suit.

Now search the poem to find answers to these questions.

1. What was Bradley doing when he fell over?

   _____

2. What animal is Jane like?

   _____

3. What noises does Jane make under the table?

   _____

4. What does Kitty do to her face?

   _____

5. Why was it hard to find Kitty during hide-and-seek?

   _____

   _____

6. **Tick the boxes** next to the clothes that Uncle Norm **did not wear** during the storm.

   coat ☐

   bathing suit ☐

   hat ☐

   boot ☐

7. Find other words that rhyme with these:

huddle _____

child _____

pretty _____

suit _____

8. Now find some different rhyming words.

Find two rhyming words in **verse 1**:

_____ rhymes with _____

Find two rhyming words in **verse 2**:

_____ rhymes with _____

Find two rhyming words in **verse 3**:

_____ rhymes with _____

Find two rhyming words in **verse 4**:

_____ rhymes with _____

THE BUG HUNT

Here are Class 2's teacher, Mrs Carter, and two children, Katie and Peter, talking about their bug hunt at school.

I'm Katie. I searched for bugs under stones. I found two worms, a slug, seven woodlice, a black beetle, a crawly thing that turned out to be a centipede, and a load of ants. It could have been an ants' nest.

Chocolate, honey, silk and strawberries: these are a few of the things we wouldn't have without bugs of one sort or another. They pollinate flowers and do a lot to tidy up too. They recycle leaves and improve the soil.

I'm Peter. I looked under a pile of dead leaves. There were a few spiders, some snails and lots of ants and woodlice. When I was about to go back to class, a shield bug landed on my sleeve. It was dark green.

1. Which **two** types of bug did both Katie and Peter find?

_____

2. Write down **three things** that we wouldn't have without bugs.

_____

3. Why did Katie find lots of ants?

_____

4. What colour was the shield bug?

_____

MOTHS

Here are some facts about the moths you might see in your garden. Remember that you don't have to memorise them. When you are answering the questions, you can read any part of it again at any time.

One way of telling a moth from a butterfly is by looking at their wings when they are resting on a leaf or on a wall.

A butterfly's wings are held up together. A moth's wings lie flat. Also, moths often have hairier bodies.

Some moths are dull grey or brown to blend in with tree bark or other plants. The moth on the right is called a Hedge Rustic. It is a good example of blending in. The colour of its wings makes it look like the bark of a tree or an old stone wall. This helps to keep it hidden from predators.

On the other hand, the moth at the top left of the page is called a Garden Tiger. It is orange-red and chocolate brown with black and white patches. These bright colours warn predators that it tastes horrid.

Both the Garden Tiger and the Hedge Rustic have long tongues to drink nectar from flowers.

People often think that butterflies are much prettier than moths. But if you spend some time looking at moths, you may be surprised at how amazing they really are.

1. How does a moth hold its wings when it is resting?

    _____

2. How is a moth's body different from a butterfly's body?

    _____

3. How does it help a moth to have a dull grey body?

    _____

    _____

4. What colour is the Garden Tiger?

    _____

    _____

5. How does the colour of the Garden Tiger help to protect it?

    _____

    _____

6. What food do moths get from flowers?

    _____

7. How do they get food from flowers?

    _____

A GUIDE TO BUTTERFLIES

Read this guide to some common butterflies, then use it to answer the questions.

 The Large White, also known as the Cabbage White, is the most common butterfly in Britain. It can be seen in gardens, parks, meadows and hedgerows. They don't always survive the British winter. They cross the English Channel every year from Southern Europe. Their caterpillars eat cabbage leaves.

The Red Admiral is easy to spot. It has red bands across its black wings. Most of them fly from Central Europe. They can be found everywhere, from the seashore to gardens to the top of mountains. Adults sip nectar from flowers. In the autumn, they eat rotting fruit. Their caterpillars eat stinging nettles.

1. What is the other name for the Large White butterfly?

_____

2. Where do most Large Whites come from?

_____

3. Where do Red Admirals come from?

_____

4. What do the caterpillars of Red Admirals eat?

_____

Here are some facts about two different butterflies.

 The Brimstone is common and is bright yellow. The word *butterfly* may have come from the idea of a butter-coloured fly. It is often the first to be seen in the year. This is because it hibernates here in woodland and comes out on warm spring days. It tends to be found in southern England.

The Painted Lady is orange and black with white spots. It is a very strong flyer. It cannot survive the British winter, but it does fly all the way from North Africa and Central Asia. Both adults and caterpillars love thistles. The adults sip the nectar and the caterpillars eat the leaves.

1.	What colour is the Brimstone butterfly?

_____

2.	In the spring, it could be the first butterfly you see. Why is that?

_____

_____

3.	What colour is the Painted Lady?

_____

4.	How do we know that the Painted Lady is a strong flyer?

_____

_____

34

ARE WE THERE, YETI?

Like all board games, this one set in the Himalayas tells you what to do whenever you land on certain numbers.

32 You've climbed Mount Everest! Congratulations!	31 You fall off the edge of a cliff. Go back four places.	30	29
25	26	27	28 Use melted icicles to make a cup of tea. Go to 30.
24 The ice bridge melts. Slip down to 17.	23	22	21
17	18	19 A yeti eats your sandwiches. Miss a turn.	20
16 A kind yeti helps you up to 20.	15	14	13 Avalanche! Go back three places.
9 You find a pair of skis. Go forward three places.	10	11 Your rope snaps. Go back to the start.	12
8	7 Yetis throw snow-balls at you. Miss a turn.	6	5
1	2	3 Yetis make faces at you. Run ahead to 6.	4

1. How many places do you have to go back if you fall off a cliff?

   _____

2. What would help you to go forward three places?

   _____

3. Which number tells you to go back three places?

   _____

4. Write down the **two** ways that yetis help you move forward.

   _____

   _____

5. Write down the **two** ways that yetis make you miss a turn.

   _____

   _____

6. What helps you move forward quickly to 30?

   _____

   _____

7. What do you have to do if your rope snaps?

   _____

THE GREAT ESCAPE

Read about the hamster, guinea pig and gerbil who got out of their cages.

Then fill in the table on page 38. Two answers have been done for you.

HARRY THE HAMSTER

GLORIA THE GUINEA PIG

GEORGE THE GERBIL

On Sunday night, when everyone in the house was snoring loudly, Harry the hamster planned his escape. He ran so fast in his hamster wheel that it smashed down the door of his cage.

George the gerbil was having the same idea. He lived in the shed. He had been keeping himself slim. So, just as Harry was breaking free, George squeezed through the bars of his cage. They met in the house at the foot of the stairs.

Harry said he was going straight to the kitchen to eat all the peanuts he could find. George wished him good luck. Instead, he went into the hallway. He chewed a hole in an old boot and hid inside. The cat saw him doing it, but when she peered inside, he bit her nose. He still hasn't been captured.

Meanwhile, Gloria the guinea pig was practising her jumping. When she was put outside in the garden in her play pen, she jumped over the side and ran off. A small boy up in his bedroom watched her through his binoculars. She crawled under the fence and chewed a hole in the neighbours' deckchair. They weren't pleased. But Gloria managed to run free for a week.

After ten days of freedom, the girl who lived in the house caught Harry in a box of cornflakes and put him back in his cage.

Now fill the boxes in this table with facts from the story.

Pet	Hamster	Guinea Pig	Gerbil
Name			
Escape plan		Gloria had been practising her jumping, so when she was put outside in the garden in her play pen, she jumped over the side.	
Where did they hide?			
Who saw them?			
When were they seen?			He was seen while he was chewing a hole in an old boot.
Free for how long?			

MARTYNA'S MYTHICAL MONSTER

Class 2 have been asked to make up their own monster before writing a monster story. This is Martyna's.

This is my monster. I don't know exactly what it is. That's why I've called it Spike. It has spikes on its back that shoot out golden lightning bolts.

It has horns on its head for protection. It doesn't have a comb, so, sometimes, its floppy hair falls in its eye and it can't see where it's going.

It's about the size of a truck. Its wings look too small for its fat body, but they can stretch out about twenty metres on each side.

It has only one big eye. It can see for miles. It can also spot really tiny bugs, which it splats with its flippers. Then it munches them.

Lots of Spike-type monsters used to fly around a long time ago in Egypt, but they kept knocking people over with their twirly tails. So they were chased away. People threw spears at them and hit them with brushes with long handles when they flew down to steal the dates off their palm trees.

I think most of them escaped to another planet. Probably Mars. You don't see many on Earth nowadays. They wear a metal triangle round their necks for sending messages to each other. They make whistling noises that we can't hear. Only dogs can hear them.

39

1. How big is Martyna's monster?

_____

2. Why is it best to stay away from the monster's spikes?

_____

3. What else does Spike use to protect itself?

_____

4. How do we know that Martyna's monster has good eyesight? Write down **two** clues.

_____

_____

5. Sometimes the monster has trouble seeing where it's going. Why?

_____

_____

6. Write down **two** things the monster likes to eat.

_____

_____

7. How big are Spike's wings?

_____

8.   Martyna says that people in Egypt got fed up of them. Why was that?

_____

_____

9.   People used **two** things to chase them away. What were they?

_____

_____

10.   Martyna says that you don't see many on Earth nowadays. Why is that?

_____

11.   What do they do with the metal triangles around their necks?

_____

12.   As well as other monsters, what other creatures can hear the whistling noises they make?

_____

13.   Martyna doesn't say anything about it swimming. Why do you think it might be good at swimming.

_____

_____

THE ALIEN PARTY

The twins, Mo and Jo, were having a birthday party together, when some aliens turned up.

Mo and Jo didn't expect aliens to come to their party. They did bring presents. That was very kind of them. Things started off all right. When they danced, everybody could hear music. It seemed to come from the sky. It even made the goldfish dance.

The game of hide-and-seek wasn't a success. Nobody could find Nish, because he had made himself invisible. We had no trouble finding Shimmer, of course. She glowed pink and green.

Gumster ruined the game of musical chairs, when he ate all the chairs. I don't think he understood the rules. Then, when we were about to have some birthday cake, Squilch zapped it with his strange eyes. What a shame. It looked delicious.

When they'd gone, Mo and Jo couldn't wait to open their presents. They looked like boxes of chocolates from another planet. It was a pity they ran away before they could be eaten.

1. How do we know that Mo and Jo didn't invite the aliens?

_____

2. What did the aliens do that was kind?

_____

3. Write down **two** unusual things about the music.

_____

_____

4. Nobody could find Nish. Why was that?

_____

5. Who glowed pink and green?

_____

6. What tells you that Gumster didn't know how to play musical chairs?

_____

7. Who ruined the birthday cake?

_____

8. Something ran away at the end. What was it?

_____

Sequence of events

Strand: Comprehension: identify and explain the sequence of events in texts

National Curriculum reference:

- discussing the sequence of events in books and how items of information are related
- checking that the text makes sense to them as they read and correcting inaccurate reading

Reading Test / Content Domain links: 1c

THE DOG AND HIS REFLECTION

Read this fable, warning us not to be greedy. Afterwards, look at the sentences below and **number** them in the right order.

A dog was very pleased to be given a bone by the butcher. It was a big bone and he hurried home as fast as he could go.

Crossing a bridge over a river, he saw himself reflected in the water. The greedy dog thought he was looking at another real dog - a dog whose bone was even bigger than his! He should have stopped to think.

Instead, he dropped his bone and leapt at the other dog. Of course, he had to swim for his life. He reached the shore and scrambled out, but he had lost his bone. He knew then how stupid he was to have been so greedy.

☐ He reached the shore and scrambled out.

☐ A dog was very pleased to have been given a bone.

☐ He should have stopped to think.

☐ He had lost his bone.

☐ He saw himself reflected in the water.

THE LION AND THE MOUSE

Here is a well-known fable. After you've read it, **number the events** below in the order in which they happened in the story.

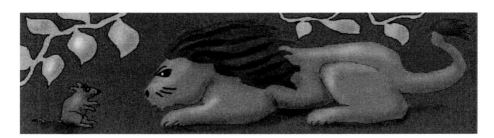

A mighty lion was sleeping in the forest, when a tiny mouse ran across his nose. Angry at being wakened up, the lion placed his heavy paw on the mouse's tail. He was ready to kill her.

"Set me free," begged the poor mouse. "One day I'll repay you."

The lion thought this was very funny. How could a mouse ever help him? But he was generous and let her go.

Some days later, the lion was caught in a hunter's net. His roar filled the forest. The mouse heard the noise and quickly found the lion struggling in the net. So she gnawed at one of the ropes that held him. Soon, he was free.

"See," said the mouse, "how even a tiny mouse can help a lion. One good turn deserves another, and kindness is never wasted."

☐ The mouse gnawed one of the ropes.

☐ The lion placed his heavy paw on the mouse's tail.

☐ The lion was caught in the hunter's net.

☐ A mighty lion was sleeping in the forest.

☐ "Set me free," begged the poor mouse.

YOUNG KING ARTHUR

Read how Arthur became king. Then **number the boxes** in the order in which things happened.

The old king died. Who should be the new king? Many people argued. No one could agree.

Then a magic stone appeared in St Paul's churchyard in London. An enormous sword was sticking in it. A message on the sword said that whoever pulled the sword from the stone was the true King of Britain.

Many strong men tried to pull the sword out, but it was stuck fast in the stone by some strange magic power. Still, no one could agree who to have as king.

When Arthur was fifteen years old, he went to London with his family. It was time for his older brother, Kay, to learn to be a knight.

Arthur was in trouble. He had forgotten to bring Kay's sword. When he went to look for one, he found the sword in the stone. He didn't know that many other men had tried to remove it. He pulled it out easily.

No one believed that Arthur had done it – not at first. So he repeated what he had done. Everyone was amazed. They had a new king: King Arthur!

Now put the events in the right order. **Number the boxes.**

[ ] Arthur went to London with his family.

[ ] Arthur became king.

[ ] The old king died.

[ ] Arthur removed the sword from the stone.

[ ] Many strong men failed to remove the sword.

[ ] Arthur went to find a sword.

[ ] A magic stone appeared in the churchyard.

THE EGG AND SPOON RACE – The Start

The teacher is trying to line up everybody for the egg and spoon race. But he's having trouble. Look at the order in which things happen.

The teacher, Mr Jackson, was about to blow his whistle to start the race. Then he saw that Eric had a real egg instead of a potato. Luckily, Mr Jackson had an extra potato handy and gave it to Eric. Everybody held up their spoons, ready to go. Then Bartek asked if he could go to the toilet. Mr Jackson nodded and looked at his watch. When Bartek returned, Samira asked if she could go as well. Mr Jackson sighed. Once everyone was lined up again, Mina dropped her potato. They all waited until she had picked it up. At last, Mr Jackson blew his whistle.

1. When Mr Jackson saw that Eric had an egg, what did he do?

_____

2. Once Eric was ready, what did everyone do?

_____

3. What did Mr Jackson do when Bartek asked to go to the toilet?

_____

4. What happened after Bartek came back?

_____

5. What happened just before Mr Jackson blew his whistle?

_____

THE EGG AND SPOON RACE – The Finishing Line

Anything can happen in an egg and spoon race. Again, here is the order in which things happened.

As soon as the race started, Mina dropped her potato again. So Eric ran off to take the lead. When he slowed down to stop his potato wobbling, Samira soon caught up with him. Suddenly, Bartek put on a burst of speed. He ran past Eric and Samira. It looked like Mina was going to be last. But Bartek fell before he reached the finishing line. Eric tripped over Bartek. Samira tripped over Eric. Mina, who was walking very slowly, passed them all and was the winner.

1.   What was the first thing that happened when the race started?

_____

2.   When did Samira catch up with Eric?

_____

_____

3.   What happened after Samira caught up with Eric?

_____

4.   Who was the first person to fall over?

_____

5.   Who was the last person to fall over?

_____

THE MISSING MONEY

This is what happened to Annie and Josh on the way to their village shop.

Mum asked Annie and Josh to go to the village shop to buy some food. Annie took the shopping list and Josh put the money in his pocket.

They crossed the road at the zebra crossing, waving to their friend, Sacha, who was playing in her garden. They said that they'd play later.

Outside the shop, they laughed as a cat chased a dog down the street. Mr Clifton, who ran the shop, smiled as they went in.

It didn't take long to fill their basket with milk, eggs and breakfast cereal. But when they went to pay, Josh had no money. It had fallen through a hole in his pocket.

Mr Clifton told them not to worry. They could pay him later. Even so, Josh and Annie were upset all the way home. Then, on the pavement outside their house, they found the money. They ran all the way back to the shop with it. Mr Clifton smiled and gave them each an ice lolly.

1. When Mum asked Annie and Josh to do some shopping, what were the first things that they did?

_____

_____

2. What did they do while they crossed the road at the crossing?

_____

3. What happened just as Annie and Josh were about to go in the shop?

_____

_____

4. What happened as soon as they went inside the shop?

_____

5. What happened just after Annie and Josh filled their basket with the shopping?

_____

_____

6. What did they do when they found the money on the pavement outside their house?

_____

_____

7. What did Mr Clifton do when they gave him the money?

_____

THE THREE LITTLE PIGS

Here is a version of the Three Little Pigs, but the parts are all mixed up.

Look for clues and **number** them so that the story is in the right order.

☐	The third little pig spent some time planning his house. Bit by bit, he built himself a skyscraper out of bricks. When it was finished, he went inside, locked the door and admired the view.
☐	When a wolf, called Mr Bad, appeared and saw the house of straw, he laughed. He huffed and puffed and blew it down so easily. The first little pig had to escape to the second pig's house.
☐	Once upon a time, there were three little pigs. "We're old enough to build our own houses," they oinked. So off they went, holding hands and skipping in the morning sunshine.
☐	Mr Bad arrived at the bungalow of sticks a few minutes later. "Let me in," he said very nicely. When the pigs refused, he blew the house of sticks down. The two pigs ran to the house of bricks.
☐	The second little pig did his best. He gathered as many sticks as he could carry. The bungalow he built wasn't as strong as he would have liked, but he was very pleased with it.
☐	Mr Bad reached the house of bricks. His mouth fell open. He coughed when he tried to blow it down. So he climbed to the top of the skyscraper, but he slipped and fell. That was the end of him.
☐	The first little pig was the laziest pig you have ever met. He piled up a load of straw and nosed his way in. He sat on a chair made of straw, with his feet on a straw stool and ate some straw.

Inferences

Strand: Make inferences from the text

National Curriculum reference:

- making inferences on the basis of what is being said and done

Reading Test / Content Domain links: 1d

HOW IS ZOE TODAY?

You can often tell how people are feeling by the way they behave. How do you think this person feels?

Tick one box.

Zoe opened the door and blushed when she saw that the room was full of people she didn't know.	shy	☐
	angry	☐
	happy	☐

When Zoe saw the present at the foot of her bed, she jumped up and down.	sorry	☐
	sad	☐
	excited	☐

Zoe didn't get on with Harriet. So when Harriet asked her to play, her mouth fell open.	cross	☐
	surprised	☐
	upset	☐

When Zoe couldn't do her homework, she stamped her foot and snapped her pencil.	sad	☐
	angry	☐
	happy	☐

WHERE IS ROBBIE TODAY?

Use the clues in these pieces of writing to work out where Robbie is. **Tick one box** under each speech bubble.

I was having lots of fun until the breeze blew sand onto my sandwiches.

The air was filled with the sound of birds and the crunch of dry leaves under my feet.

North Pole ☐

beach ☐

ocean ☐

beach ☐

rocket ship ☐

forest ☐

My nose was itching terribly, but I didn't dare take off my thick, furry gloves.

I've never been so excited. I could see the tiny moon and how blue the Earth was.

Wherever I looked, there was no sign of land – just miles and miles of water.

forest ☐

North Pole ☐

rocket ship ☐

North Pole ☐

ocean ☐

rocket ship ☐

ocean ☐

beach ☐

forest ☐

✦ SUPER PENGUIN ✦

John looks like an ordinary penguin

But when he removes his hat and glasses...

A text comes in – someone needs ... SUPER PENGUIN!

A nasty shark is after some cuddly penguins left all alone

Super Penguin grabs the shark and drags him miles away

The cuddly penguins send him another text...

1. Why do you think Super Penguin calls himself John and wears a hat and glasses?

_____

_____

2. What happens when he takes off his hat and glasses?

_____

3. Why does he need a cloak to fly?

_____

4. Why does he need to be faster than a rocket?

_____

_____

5. He can breathe without air. Where would that be useful?

_____

_____

6. In the third picture, he looks very serious. Why do you think that is?

_____

7. Picture 4 makes it clear who the good guys are and who the bad guy is. How does it do that?

_____

_____

8.	What super power has Super Penguin used in picture 4?

_____

9.	Which of his super powers is Super Penguin using in picture 5?

_____

_____

10.	Why do you think the other two sharks are looking worried?

_____

_____

11.	In the last picture why does he say: "**This is worrying!**"?

_____

_____

_____

L. S. LOWRY

Read this information about the British painter, Laurence Stephen Lowry. To answer the questions that follow, you'll have to use the clues in the text.

Artist – L. S. Lowry

Laurence was born in 1887. As a child, he did not have many friends. His mother had dreamt of becoming a famous pianist, but her health was bad after he was born.

As a young boy, he lived on the edge of Manchester surrounded by trees. This became too expensive. The family had to move house. Then Laurence had to get used to seeing the smoke from factory chimneys rather than trees. Later, this was to become part of his art.

After leaving school, he studied art. He was interested in painting the landscape of factories, football crowds and working people that surrounded him. He is often described as painting 'matchstick men'.

His mother, who was ill for some time, died in 1939, before she could see how successful he had become.

He died in 1976. By then, he had done over 1000 paintings and 8000 drawings. Thirty-five years later, in 2011, one of his paintings sold for five million pounds.

1. Do you think Laurence had a happy childhood?

    _____ ✏

2. Why do you think that?

    _____

    _____

3. What words tell you that Laurence's mother was longing to be a great pianist?

    _____

4. How do you know the family was not rich?

    _____

    _____

5. How did Laurence make use of the factories he saw around him?

    _____

6. Laurence's mother never saw what a famous artist he became. Why was that?

    _____

    _____

7. How do we know he spent a lot of time painting?

    _____

    _____

MY VISIT TO THE TAJ MAHAL

Meera has just returned from a holiday in India, where she visited the Taj Mahal. Here she is talking about it.

The Taj Mahal is so beautiful. It's a kind of tomb in India for somebody special who passed away. I know I'd never be able to afford to build one. We made a special trip to the city of Agra to see it, because it's world-famous. It's right next to the River Yamuna. We were told that the Emperor Shah Jahan had it built for his wife, Mumtaz Mahal. It took 20 years to finish. This was round about 1653. They say that poets compared it to a white cloud. It's made of white marble, which gleamed as the sun rose!

1. What does Meera say that lets us know that she liked the Taj Mahal?

_____

2. What sort of building is the Taj Mahal?

_____

3.   Instead of saying a tomb is for people who have died, what does she say?

   _____

4.   How do we know that Meera thinks you'd have to be rich to build one?

   _____

5.   Meera says the Taj Mahal is very well-known. What words does she use?

   _____

6.   Meera visited the Taj Mahal early in the morning. How do we know?

   _____

   _____

7.   Poets must have thought it was amazing. How do we know?

   _____

Predicting what might happen

Strand: Making inferences: predict what might happen on the basis of what has been read so far

National Curriculum reference:

- predicting what might happen on the basis of what has been read so far

Reading Test / Content Domain links: 1e

FIX THE FAIRYTALE

Draw lines to join up what happens in these sentences from fairytales.

One has been done for you.

Jack's mother threw the beans out of the window.	The wolf blew the house down.
The first pig built a house made of straw.	She turned the mice into white horses.
Princess Beauty pricked her finger.	The wolf pretended to be her grandmother.
The fairy godmother waved her magic wand.	In the night, a huge beanstalk grew.
Snow White fell asleep in the cottage.	Birds flew down and ate the bread.
Little Red Riding Hood knocked on the door.	Everyone in the castle fell asleep.
Hansel and Gretel left a trail of crumbs.	The seven little men were very surprised.

WHAT'S FOR DINNER?

This text describes a food chain. It tells you what some animals eat. Read it carefully and try to write in the missing words.

A Food Chain

Everything that is alive needs energy. Energy comes from food. Plants make their own _____, by using the sun, air and water. Animals can't make their own food.

At the start of a food chain there is usually a plant. An animal eats the plant, then it gets eaten by a bigger _____, and so on. For example, a slug eats a _____. A hedgehog eats the _____. A fox then comes along and eats the _____. Some animals, such as cows and sheep, only eat plants. Some animals, such as lions and tigers, only eat meat. Other animals, such as human beings, eat both _____ and _____.

When you are drawing a food _____ like the picture above, remember that the arrow means:

is eaten by

SEEING THE FUTURE

What do you think happened to these children? There are clues in the sentences. Finish them off.

1. When Ruth was feeding the ducks in the pond, she went too close to the edge and...

    _____

2. Trying to pull the carrot out of the ground, Toby heaved and heaved, until suddenly...

    _____

3. Freddie loved the look of his birthday cake, so, when his mother left the kitchen,...

    _____

4. Standing on a chair, Jen was sure she could reach the last apple high in the tree, but...

    _____

    _____

5. In the night, the garden path froze, so when Joe ran outside, he...

    _____

    _____

6. Running out of the door, Anya bumped into her father carrying a huge...

_____

_____

7. When Jamil took his dog for a walk on the beach, the dog...

_____

_____

8. Paddling their canoe on the lake, Abdel and Rebekka...

_____

_____

9. Katrina laughed so much when she heard Aneta's joke that...

_____

_____

10. Sam was looking forward so much to a picnic with Grandad. But when the picnic basket was opened...

_____

_____

TREASURE MAP

You need to know which way to go if you head north, south, east or west.

If you don't, you won't find the treasure. Use this map and read the clues.

TREASURE MAP – clues

Here are your clues. Use them to make sense of the map.

ORC COUNTRY

The orcs are not very clever, but they are very good at guarding the way to Fairy Land. They won't let you walk through their country unless you have the secret password. Only wizards know what it is.

WIZARD CORNER

The wizard hides the secret password under his scruffy old hat. He never gives anything away unless he gets something in return. He hasn't had a new hat for 683 years.

DRAGON ISLAND

Deep inside a dark cave, protected by a dragon, there is the treasure. The island is in the middle of the Crocodile Sea. So you can't swim there.

FAIRY LAND

The fairies can do all sorts of things. They can make crocodiles go to sleep, but they are scared of dark caves and dragons. They also have a spell that can make magic ponies fly as high as the clouds.

MAGIC PONY FIELDS

The magic ponies are quite lonely and long for a day when they can let someone ride them around their fields. They often stare up at the sky and wonder what is up there.

CLOUDLAND

In Cloudland, there lives an old man. He can float on a cloud and has the power to make dragons do anything he wants just by looking at them. He could get you the treasure, but he is afraid of the dark.

---

1. If you walk west from your starting point (**You are here**), who will you meet?

_____

2. When a fairy looks to the south, what does she see?

_____

3. Do you see where the middle crocodile is? When it faces east, which land does it see?

_____

4. If you asked an orc what he was good at, what do you think he would say?

_____

5. Where does the wizard keep the secret password?

_____

6. If you tried to swim to where the treasure is hidden, what do you think might happen to you?

_____

_____

7.   Write down **two** reasons why the fairies would not go and get the treasure for you.

_____

_____

8.   What would happen if you tried to ride a magic pony?

_____

9.   If the old man from Cloudland came face to face with a fierce dragon, what do you think he would do?

_____

_____

10.   Using the map and the clues, work out a way of getting the treasure.

_____

_____

_____

_____

_____

_____

FINISH THE FABLE

A fable is a story that teaches a lesson. This is usually called the **moral**.

Here are short examples of fables. Using the clues in the moral, write

down how you think the fable might end.

The Oak Tree and the Reeds

An oak tree was very proud. It was so pleased that it did not bend in
the wind like the reeds. The reeds said that they might bend, but they
never broke. The oak tree laughed at the reeds. But then the wind
turned into a hurricane.

_____

_____

Moral: Pride comes before a fall.

The Wolf and its Shadow

One evening, a wolf saw its shadow. With
the sun low on the horizon, its shadow was
very big. It was so amazed by how huge it
was, it called out: "I should be the King of the
Beasts; not the lion!" Then another, even
bigger shadow appeared.

_____

_____

_____

Moral: Only the fool has a high opinion of
himself.

FURTHER FABLES

Here are two more fables to finish off.

The Boy Who Cried Wolf

A shepherd boy grew bored looking after the sheep. He thought he would have some fun by crying: "Wolf! Wolf!" The villagers ran to save him. Of course, there was no wolf and the boy laughed. He did this several times. Each time, the villagers came running. Then one day, a wolf really did appear.

_____

_____

_____

Moral: No one believes a liar even when they tell the truth.

The Grasshopper and the Ants

All summer, the ants were busy storing food for the winter. The grasshopper poked fun at them for working so hard. He was happy playing his fiddle. Autumn came and grasshopper still fiddled. Then the cold winds of winter arrived.

_____

_____

_____

_____

Moral: There is time for work and time for play.

Features of texts and meaning

Strand: Comprehension / Themes and Conventions

National Curriculum reference:

- being introduced to non-fiction books that are structured in different ways
- explaining and discussing their understanding of books, poems and other material, both those that they listen to and those that they read for themselves
- becoming increasingly familiar with and retelling a wider range of stories, fairy stories and traditional tales

Not part of the reading test, but consolidated in KS2 as 2f.

CARNIVAL MASK

Here is a page about making the kind of mask worn during Carnival time in South American countries such as Brazil. Read the information in each box and write a title on each line. Then, answer the questions.

Brazilians love Carnival. It takes place six weeks before Easter and lasts for six days. There is music, singing and dancing. There are lots of parades in which people dress up in fancy costumes and colourful masks.

Get the following things ready:
- pencil and drawing paper to explore different mask shapes
- a piece of card as wide as your head
- scissors
- string or elastic
- coloured pencils, paints, crayons and feathers

Once you have a mask design you like, draw it onto the card. Cut it out with the scissors. Holding it against your face, ask a friend to mark it with a pencil where the eye holes should be. Cut out the eye holes. Make two holes on each side of the mask. Tie the string through these new holes so that the mask stays in place on your face. Decorate with the coloured pencils, crayons or paint and feathers.

1. How long does Carnival last?

   _____

2. During a parade, how might people be dressed?

   _____

3. Why should you get coloured pencils, paints, crayons and feathers ready?

   _____

   _____

4. What is the next thing you do after you've drawn a mask shape that you like?

   _____

5. What should you do just before you cut out the eyeholes?

   _____

   _____

6. Why do you think the writer has added some pictures of masks?

   _____

   _____

   _____

THE PENGUIN

Here is a page out of an information book about penguins. See how the picture of the penguin has labels to help you read the facts.

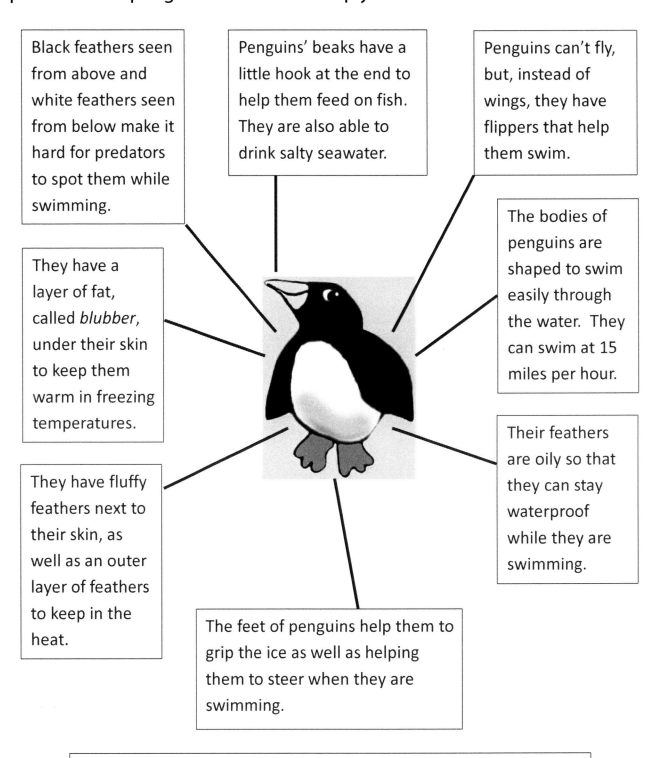

Black feathers seen from above and white feathers seen from below make it hard for predators to spot them while swimming.

Penguins' beaks have a little hook at the end to help them feed on fish. They are also able to drink salty seawater.

Penguins can't fly, but, instead of wings, they have flippers that help them swim.

The bodies of penguins are shaped to swim easily through the water. They can swim at 15 miles per hour.

They have a layer of fat, called *blubber*, under their skin to keep them warm in freezing temperatures.

Their feathers are oily so that they can stay waterproof while they are swimming.

They have fluffy feathers next to their skin, as well as an outer layer of feathers to keep in the heat.

The feet of penguins help them to grip the ice as well as helping them to steer when they are swimming.

They also huddle together to stay warm. As many as 5000 penguins will crowd close together when freezing winds are blowing.

1. How fast can a penguin swim?

   _____

2. Penguins are fast swimmers. Write down **two** things that help them.

   _____

   _____

3. How is being black and white good for the penguin?

   _____

   _____

4. What do penguins drink?

   _____

5. Which part of the penguin's body helps it to steer while it is swimming?

   _____

6. Write down **three** things that help a penguin stay warm.

   _____

   _____

   _____

LOST IN THE GARDEN

Here is a poem that wanders around different parts of a garden.

? I know I had it yesterday

And dropped it by the tree.

I suppose it could have rolled away.

Wherever can it be?

Perhaps it's underneath that nettle.

I'll try and not be stung.

Or possibly it came to settle

Where the washing has been hung.

Or over by the compost heap,

Or near the climbing rose,

In the bush where robins cheep

And prickly holly grows.

I'll have to live without it now,

Though it came from Santa Claus.

Oh, well. Never mind. You know, somehow,

I've forgotten what it was!

1. The first verse gives you a hint that the shape of the thing that's lost is round. Write down the words that tell you.

_____

_____

2. How might the writer be stung?

_____

_____

3. What other plant in the poem might hurt the writer?

_____

4. Name **two** parts of the garden in the poem that are not plants.

_____

_____

5. There are two big question marks on the page – one at the beginning and one at the end. What are the **two questions** being asked in this poem?

_____

_____

_____

MOUNT EVEREST

On this page from a non-fiction book about mountains, each box of information has been given a heading. It makes it easier to find the answers you're looking for.

MOUNT EVEREST

How big and how old?

Mount Everest, between Nepal, Tibet and China, is 29,035 feet high or 8848 metres and it grows higher by about ½ cm every year. It is over 60 million years old.

The mountain's history

People in Europe and the USA didn't know much about the mountain until George Everest studied it in 1841. It was named Mount Everest in 1865.

Who's been to the top?

The first climbers to reach the summit were Edmund Hillary from New Zealand and Tenzing Norgay from Nepal on 29th May, 1953. The youngest to climb it are Jordan Romero from America (22nd May, 2010) and Malavath Poorna from India (25th May, 2014). They were both 13 years old when they reached the highest point.

What's the weather like?

At the top of the mountain it can be as cold as -60° C. Sometimes, the wind reaches a speed of 200mph. In May and October, however, it is warmer and calmer. This is the time that climbers try to reach the summit. From June to September, the mountain can be covered in mist with dangerous floods and mud slides.

1. How high is Mount Everest?

   _____

2. How old is Mount Everest?

   _____

3. What part did George Everest play in the history of the mountain?

   _____

   _____

4. What word in the text means **the top of the mountain?**

   _____

5. Who were the first people to reach the top?

   _____

   _____

6. When did the first people reach the top?

   _____

7. What was the name of the teenage boy who made it to the top?

   _____

8. Malavath Poorna got to the top of Everest when she was 13 years old. What country was she from?

_____

9. How cold can it be on Mount Everest?

_____

10. 200mph is mentioned. What is this?

_____

11. Which months are the safest months to climb the mountain?

_____

12. Why is it dangerous to try to climb Everest in the middle of summer?

_____

_____

What about the yetis?

Words that capture the reader's imagination

Strand: Language for effect

National Curriculum reference:

- discussing their favourite words and phrases

- recognising simple recurring literary language in stories and poetry

- developing pleasure in reading, motivation to read, vocabulary and understanding by: listening to, discussing and expressing views about a wide range of contemporary and classic poetry, stories and non-fiction at a level beyond that at which they can read independently

Not part of the reading test, but consolidated in KS2 as 2g.

FIND THE RHYMES

Look for the rhymes in this poem and listen to the galloping rhythm.

GALLOPING STILL

This is the horse that couldn't wait
To see the world, so jumped the gate,
Swam the river and climbed the hill.
With so much to see, it's galloping still.

This is the dog whose work was a bore.
Guarding the sheep, it dreamt of much more.
It leapt on the horse that couldn't wait
To see the world, so jumped the gate,
Swam the river and climbed the hill.
With so much to see, it's galloping still.

This is the cat, so weary of mice,
Wished for adventure and didn't think twice,
So hopped on the dog whose work was a bore.
Guarding the sheep, it dreamt of much more.
It leapt on the horse that couldn't wait
To see the world, so jumped the gate,
Swam the river and climbed the hill.
With so much to see, it's galloping still.

This is the crow that flew at the cat
Sending the dog to the ground with a SPLAT!
Leaving the horse way over the hill.
With so much to see, it's galloping still.

1. What are the **three** things the horse does when it goes off to see the world?

_____

_____

_____

2. Why does the dog join the horse?

_____

_____

3. Why does the cat join the horse and the dog?

_____

_____

Now find the words that rhyme with these:

word	rhyme
still	
wait	
more	
mice	
cat	

ONE THING LIKE ANOTHER

We have lots of sayings, comparing one thing to another, such as: **as busy as a bee**. **Draw lines** to make the saying complete. One has already been done for you.

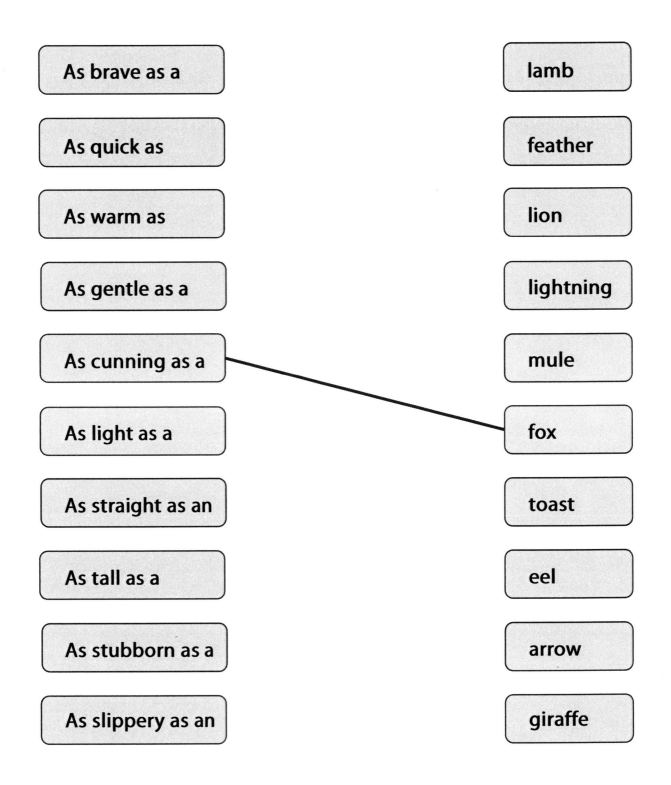

As brave as a	lamb
As quick as	feather
As warm as	lion
As gentle as a	lightning
As cunning as a	mule
As light as a	fox
As straight as an	toast
As tall as a	eel
As stubborn as a	arrow
As slippery as an	giraffe

PICTURE THIS

Look at this picture. Below, parts of the picture are compared to other things. **Tick the sentence** that you think is right, then say **why** you chose that one.

1. Does the moon look like a...   **smile**

    or a...   **balloon?**

    Why did you tick that one?

    _____

2. Do the fireworks look like a...   **fountain**

    or...   **flowers?**

    Why did you tick that one?

    _____

3. Do the bats look like...   **black hats**

    or...   **black umbrellas?**

    Why did you tick that one?

    _____

THE UNICORN HUNT

Here is a poem about following some magical footprints.

HUNTING THE UNICORN

Down in the forest where the stinkwort grows,
Rosalind the Elf is holding her nose.
She's following footprints left in the snow
That glimmer and shimmer with a silver glow.

They wind round trees and pass through stone,
Taking the elf to a place unknown.
Here, buttercups melt and dragonflies sing,
And toadstools laugh at the silliest thing.

This is no place for you and me,
With its spells and magic and dark mystery.
But the elf seeks to touch the golden horn
Of the fabulous beast called the unicorn.

She tracks and searches for a year and a day
Till all trace of the creature fades right away.
But Rosalind turns when the evergreens stir
To find the unicorn following her.

1. What is the name of the plant that makes Rosalind hold her nose?

_____

2. What do you notice about the words **glimmer** and **shimmer**?

_____

3. Look at verse 1. What is magical about the footprints?

_____

4. Look at verse 2. What else is strange about the footprints?

_____

5. Write down **two** of the things in verse 2 that can't really happen.

_____

_____

6. Why is Rosalind the Elf trying to find the unicorn?

_____

7. Something happens to Rosalind at the end that she doesn't expect. What is it?

_____

_____

TORNADOES

This description of tornadoes is non-fiction. Even so, the writer has used some interesting words to give the reader some idea of what a tornado is like.

Tornadoes

A tornado is a spinning tunnel of air that stretches from the bottom of a cloud down to the Earth. A common name for a tornado in America is *twister.*

Most tornadoes travel a few miles before dying out. More powerful tornadoes can travel over 100 miles and destroy houses.

In 1925, the deadliest tornado in the history of the USA started off as a 'smoky fog' then travelled 219 miles and killed 695 people.

Most tornadoes take place in the middle of the USA. Because of this, the area is known as Tornado Alley. Here, there are more tornadoes than anywhere else in the world: around 1200 in a year. But the world's most violent tornado occurred in Bangladesh in 1989, killing 1300 people.

Some reporters and photographers will chase tornadoes in order to get good pictures of them. They are known as *tornado hunters.* The safest place to be during this kind of violent storm is down in a basement or cellar. Don't stand near a window. Sometimes, they can travel at 60 mph. So don't go outside unless you drive in the opposite direction.

1. What is the common name given to a tornado in America?

   _____

2. Why is this a good name for a tornado?

   _____

   _____

3. How far can more powerful tornadoes travel?

   _____

4. When did the **deadliest tornado** take place in the USA?

   _____

5. What did it look like when it started off?

   _____

6. What name is given to the part of the USA where tornadoes are common?

   _____

7. Where did the world's most violent tornado take place?

   _____

8. What name is given to people who chase tornadoes?

   _____

PLEASE NOTE:

The digital version also contains the book and tests filed separately for printing. A full answer version and colour digital versions of the book and tests are also included.

The raw score/scaled score conversion charts are also supplied.

Strand: Range of texts

National Curriculum objectives:

- [listening to and] discussing a wide range of fiction, poetry, plays, non-fiction and reference books or textbooks

- reading books that are structured in different ways and reading for a range of purposes

- increasing their familiarity with a wide range of books, including fairy stories, myths and legends [and retelling some of these orally]

Reading Test / Content Domain links: 1a, 1b, 1c, 1d, 1e

A note about the tests:

The KS1 English Reading Test Framework 2016 (table 9) sets out the proportion of marks for each domain, with the higher percentages given to **retrieving and recording information** and **making inferences**. This is reflected in the test questions presented here.

Pupils working at the expected standard are able to:

- identify the meaning of vocabulary in context (**1a**)
- retrieve and explain relevant details from fiction and non-fiction to demonstrate understanding of characters, events and information (**1b**)
- identify sequences of events in a range of straightforward texts (**1c**)
- make simple and general inferences based on the text (**1d**)
- make simple and general predictions based on the text (**1e**)

As can be seen from the above set of points, the statutory reading comprehension test at Key Stage 1 does not cover every aspect of the national curriculum for English. The ongoing assessment of other important aspects of literacy, such as the features of different genres and language that capture the imagination, is the responsibility of teachers.

HeadStart
primary

Year 2 Reading Comprehension - Test Admin Guidance

Before Starting the Test

Explain to the children that the questions require different kinds of answers.

The space for the answer shows the type of answer required. Some questions require a one word/short answer and others require a longer answer.

For some questions, a different type of answer is required e.g. circling/ticking an answer or joining two items together with a line.

The number underneath the line on the right-hand side of each question indicates how many marks there are for each question.

Timing

The Year 2 tests are not intended to be strictly timed tests, so please allow as much time as necessary. If appropriate, the tests can be stopped and re-started as long as pupils do not have a chance to share/discuss the test content. It may be appropriate to split a test over two or more sessions.

Equipment

Each pupil will need a pencil or pen.

A rubber can be used but crossing out is preferable as long as answers remain legible.

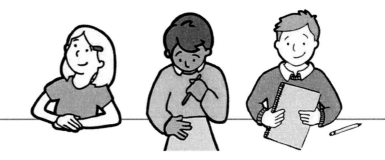

Assistance

General instructions on the test papers may be read to children. Instructions may also be re-phrased as long as no inappropriate assistance is given.

In Year 2, it may be appropriate for some children to read the texts and questions aloud if this is part of normal classroom practice. This should happen in a different room than children completing the tests silently.

Children with Special Needs or Disabilities

If children need specific kinds of assistance, equipment or environment to complete the tests, this should be provided as long as it is part of normal classroom practice.

HeadStart
primary

Reading Comprehension

YEAR 2

Scaled Score TEST A

Name: ....

Class: ....

Date: ....

Raw Score .... / 40

Scaled Score ....

CAN'T DO ANYTHING

It's time for school. Ramal's little sister, Tara, says, "Can I come?"

"No," says Ramal. "You're too little."

"You can take my rag doll," says Tara.

Ramal rolls his eyes around. "What? I don't need a doll. I'm big now." Tara and his mother wave him goodbye as he runs off to school.

1 Ramal tells Tara she can't go to school. Why?

....

1 mark

2 Tara is kind. How do you know?

....

....

1 mark

3 Why does Ramal **roll his eyes around**? **Tick one box.**

he is feeling ill ☐

he's annoyed ☐

he's doing a trick ☐

1 mark

Page Total

At the end of the lane, he meets the twins, Mo and Jo. They've brought their skipping ropes to play with.

Along the winding road near the trees, Ramal hears a roaring sound. It's Alex. He's brought an aeroplane made of twigs and leaves to play with.

As Ramal crosses the bridge over the river, he meets Connie talking to herself. She has a cuddly toy elephant to play with.

At school, the teacher says, "At school today you can all play with your toys."

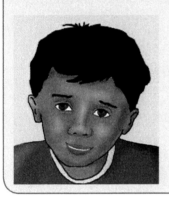

Ramal looks upset. He doesn't have anything, not even Tara's rag doll. The teacher sees he has nothing to play with. Because she's very kind, she says, "Let's make a toy!" Everyone cheers. Ramal smiles a tiny bit.

4 Ramal meets his friends. **Draw lines** to join the names of his friends to the place where he meets them.

Mo and Jo	**winding road**
Connie	**end of the lane**
Alex	**bridge over the river**

2 marks

2

Page Total

5 In the story, who likes to skip?

....

1 mark

6 Alex made his own aeroplane. What did he make it out of?

....

1 mark

7 Who owns the toy elephant?

....

1 mark

8 **'Ramal looks upset.'**

Circle one word that means the same as **upset**.

bored   tired   sad

1 mark

9 The children are happy when the teacher says,

"Let's make a toy."

How do you know they are happy?

....

....

1 mark

3

Page Total

Everyone gets some wood. Ramal picks up a hammer. He spends a lot of time missing his block of wood. "I can't do anything," he says.

Connie makes a wooden dolphin. It floats. Ramal's floats too. But it just looks like a floating piece of wood.

Alex makes a mobile. Ramal holds his up high too. But when he lets it go, it hits the floor with a ... BUMP!

The twins, Mo and Jo, make a little car with wooden wheels. Ramal races his toy against theirs. It doesn't move because it's just a chunk of wood.

"I can't do anything," he mutters. He wishes he had taken Tara's rag doll to school after all.

10 What tool does Ramal use to make his toy?

....

1 mark

11 The children make different toys. Draw lines matching the children to their toys.

Mo and Jo	mobile
Connie	dolphin
Alex	car

2 marks

Page Total

So Ramal kicks his bad lump of wood all the way home. It bounces across the bridge. It smacks into the rocks. He picks it up and kicks it again. It bounces off the trees. It tumbles along the winding road.

He kicks it until it's dented and battered. When he gets home, he drops it onto the table. Tara picks up the lump of wood. "Can I have this toy?" she asks.

Ramal is surprised. After all the kicking and bouncing and rolling and denting, the block of wood has a new shape. The bad toy looks just like a hippo made of wood.

His mother says, "What a clever Ramal you are!"

Ramal smiles and nods.

12 On the way home, Ramal kicks his chunk of wood off different things. **Number the boxes**, putting the different things in the right order.

One has been done for you.

☐	**trees**
☐	**winding road**
1	**bridge**
☐	**rocks**

2 marks

Page Total

13 Why is Ramal surprised when Tara picks up the piece of wood?

....

....

1 mark

14 Find **two** other words used in the story that mean the same as **piece** of wood.

1. .... **of wood**

2. .... **of wood**

1 mark

15 When Ramal goes to school the next day, what do you think he'll say to his friends?

....

....

....

....

2 marks

Page Total

THE RUBBISH BAND

Gongs are big and made of metal. You strike them with a beater. They can be deafening, so, long ago in China, they beat them to tell farmers to come for dinner. I made mine from one of Mum's old baking trays. Dad drilled two holes in the top. I added stickers and tied it to a twig. The beater is a wooden spoon with tape wrapped round it. Mum wants it back afterwards.

TAKISHA

1 Long ago in China, why did they use gongs?

....

....

1 mark

2 What does **deafening** mean? **Circle one**.

loud   **quiet**   **scary**

1 mark

3 Write down **two** ways that Mum and Dad helped Takisha to make her own gong.

1. ....

2. ....

2 marks

7

Page Total

4 Why do you think Takisha added stickers?

....

....

1 mark

5 Why do you think Takisha's mother wants the beater back afterwards?

....

....

2 marks

FREDDIE

They used rainsticks in South America to ask the spirits to make it rain. They made them out of dead cactus. This one is a cardboard tube. I taped brown paper to one end. Inside, I put in a long piece of twisted tin foil, then some rice and dried pasta. I taped more paper over the other end, then I painted it. When you turn it upside down, the stuff inside trickles down. It sounds like rain.

6 What did they use rainsticks for in South America?

....

....

1 mark

8

Page Total

7 What were South American rainsticks made out of?
Circle one.

cardboard   cactus   wood

1 mark

8 Here is a list of what Freddie did when he made his
rainstick. **Number** them in the correct order.
One has already been done for you.

☐	**taped brown paper over one end**
1	**found a cardboard tube**
☐	**decorated it**
☐	**taped paper over the other end**
☐	**put in twisted tin foil**
☐	**put in rice and dried pasta**

2 marks

9 How do you make the rainstick sound like rain?

....

....

....

2 marks

Page Total

All our instruments are made from rubbish. Grandad gave me a plastic pipe he didn't need. Using a saw, I cut it into different sizes - short, long and some in between. Then, using scissors, I cut roundish shapes out of a cardboard box for the pipes to sit in. When you strike them, they make different notes. The band's not very good yet. We are rubbish, but we will get better.

TOM

10 Read what Tom says about the instrument he made.
What does it remind you of? **Circle one**.

drum   trumpet   xylophone

1 mark

11 Tom used **two** tools. What were they?

1. ....

2. ....

2 marks

12 Who gave Tom the plastic pipe?

....

1 mark

Page Total

13 Why did Tom cut the pipe into different sizes?

....

....

1 mark

14 Look again at what all three children say.

Who **did not** use any cardboard when they made

their instrument?

....

1 mark

15 There are **two** reasons why the writer used the title,

The Rubbish Band. What are the **two** reasons?

1. ....

....

2. ....

....

2 marks

End of TEST A

HeadStart
primary

Reading Comprehension

YEAR 2

Scaled Score TEST B

Name: ....

Class: ....

Date: ....

Raw Score ..../40

Scaled Score ....

THE SLOW-WORM

WHAT IS IT?

It might be called a slow-worm, but it's not a worm and it's not slow. It might look like a snake, but it isn't. It's a lizard that has no legs. Like other lizards, it has eyelids and can blink. Also, like lizards, when it is attacked, it can leave its tail behind and escape.

1 What is odd about the slow-worm's name?
Find and copy **two** things.

1. ....

2. ....

2 marks

2 Read what it says about the slow-worm and **tick** the

sentences that are **true**.

It is a snake. ☐

It has no legs. ☐

It can blink. ☐

1 mark

Page Total ○

WHAT DOES IT LOOK LIKE?

The slow-worm is smaller than a snake, with very shiny, silvery-pink skin. The female is bigger than the male. She has darker sides and a dark stripe down the back. The male is paler and sometimes has blue spots. Both have very smooth skin and are between 30 cm and 40 cm long. A slow-worm can live for 20 years.

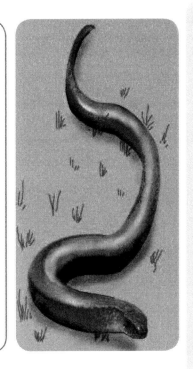

3 Read these sentences. After each one, **draw a circle** round **true** or **false**.

The male is bigger than the female.	true	false
The female has a dark stripe down its back.	true	false
The male sometimes has blue spots.	true	false
Both male and female can live up to 30 years.	true	false

2 marks

4 How long is a slow-worm? **Tick one.**

between 20 cm and 30 cm ☐

between 30 cm and 40 cm ☐

1 mark

Page Total

WHERE MIGHT YOU SEE ONE?

They can be spotted on rough grassland or at the edge of woodland. That's where they feed on slugs, snails and some insects. If you're lucky, you might see one in your compost heap or sunbathing in your garden. Being a reptile, they need the sun to warm up their bodies. Look for them in spring, when they come out of hibernation.

REMEMBER

A slow-worm will not hurt you. It's against the law to kill or harm one of these beautiful creatures.

5 Find and write down **three** places where you might spot a slow-worm.

1. ....

2. ....

3. ....

2 marks

6 Write down **one** thing they like to eat.

....

1 mark

7 Why is spring a good time to see a slow-worm?

....

....

1 mark

8 Write down the sentence that means:

Slow-worms are harmless.

....

....

1 mark

THE NIGHT PATROL

Here is a poem about animals that come out at night.

THE NIGHT PATROL

Buzz, whistle, creak, hoot -
We're the guys who dare set foot
Into the dark after vole and mole.
We're all members of the Night Patrol.

Hear the screech of the wide-eyed owl,
Or watch the badgers on the prowl.
Here is the whine, here is the bark
Of fox - a master of the dark.

1 Write down **three** words that sound like animal noises.

1. ....

2. ....

3. ....

1 mark

2 Find and copy a word that rhymes with **patrol**.

....

1 mark

Page Total

3 Write down the words that describe how well the owl can see in the dark.

....

1 mark

4 Which animal is described as **master of the dark**?

....

1 mark

5 Number these animals in the order they come in the poem.

owl

vole

fox

badger

2 marks

Page Total

We swoop and leap to catch our prey.
Did rabbit and vole get clean away?
Did the watchful mouse come under attack?
Did the moth meet the bat and become its snack?

When the sun comes up, it's time to relax.
Let the bending flowers cover our tracks.
But, remember, at night, who's in control.
Yes, us - sneaky members of the Night Patrol.

6 Write down **two** words from verse 3 that describe how animals move when they are hunting.

1. ....

2. ....

1 mark

7 Write down **three** animals that are hunted at night.

1. ....

2. ....

3. ....

2 marks

Page Total

NOCTURNAL ANIMALS

Nocturnal animals are those that come out mostly at night to find food. Use the table below to answer the questions about nocturnal animals.

animal	food	habitat	predators	notes
badger	mice, eggs, roots and up to 200 worms a day	badgers live underground in a sett with lots of exits	cubs eaten by buzzards or foxes - also killed on roads	badgers have sharp claws for digging
dormouse	flowers, fruits, nuts and insects	curled up in a ball of grass and leaves	dormice are eaten by owls and foxes	large eyes - also long tail for balance
owl	mice, moles, voles, frogs, lizards, insects, small birds	owls like old barns and hollow trees	owls are not hunted and eaten by other animals	owls have strong talons for grabbing hold of prey
bat	flying insects - as much as 3000 a night	trees, caves, barns, houses and bridges	bats are eaten by owls, cats and snakes	uses echo of high-pitched squeak to catch insects
hedgehog	slugs, snails, insects, eggs, frogs	under hedges, in woods or fields	eaten by foxes, badgers and owls	500 or more fleas live on hedgehogs
fox	foxes eat birds, rats, mice, slugs, insects and human food waste	underground, in woodland, fields or gardens	foxes have no natural predators - only human hunters	good night vision - its bushy tail is called a 'brush'

1 How many worms can a badger eat in one day?

....

1 mark

2 How many fleas might be living on a hedgehog?

....

1 mark

3 Which animal has a bushy tail called a **brush**?

....

1 mark

4 What is special about a badger's claws?

....

....

1 mark

5 **Owls have strong talons for grabbing hold of prey.**

What are **talons**? **Tick one.**

claws ☐

skills ☐

eyesight ☐

1 mark

Page Total

6 Look down the **food** column. Which **three** animals eat mice?

1. ....

2. ....

3. ....

2 marks

7 Look at the box that tells you what dormice eat.

Tick one thing it does **not** eat.

insects ☐   frogs ☐   flowers ☐

1 mark

8 **Circle** the animal that is **not** hunted by other animals.

bat   owl   hedgehog

1 mark

9 **Draw lines** to join each animal to where it lives.

badger   barn

bat   hedgerow

hedgehog   underground

1 mark

Page Total

A LOVELY DAY FOR A PICNIC

"Not a cloud in the sky!" That's what Dad said. That's how it all started. What a disaster! But quite funny really.

It all happened last Saturday. I'm Sian. I don't enjoy being dragged out of bed at six o'clock in the morning, even if it is great picnic weather.

Dad was being very cheerful. He was helping Mum make sandwiches. Well, in the time it took Mum to make four tuna and two egg sandwiches, Dad managed to make one cheese sandwich. Then he dropped it on the floor. Luckily, our dog, Charlie, likes cheese.

I asked about the strange clonking noise as we drove into the countryside.

"Oh, it's nothing, Sian," said Dad, a few seconds before the car broke down. Luckily, we were close to the woods. Dad just smiled as he threw all the picnic stuff into his rucksack and marched off. "Come on," he said. "This is the way." I looked down at Charlie – we weren't so sure.

We wandered around lost for an hour, looking for the picnic spot beside the lake. When Dad stopped to check the map on his phone, he dropped it down a rabbit hole. I wondered what the rabbits would think of that.

It was a pity Dad tripped over the stone and fell backwards into the marsh. That was all the food ruined. It was a long walk back home. We all felt tired, disappointed and hungry. It was a lovely, sunny day too. Pity about the sunburn.

11

1 Dad said to Sian it was lovely weather for a picnic.

What words did he use to describe the weather?

....

.... 1 mark

2 What time did Sian have to get out of bed?

.... 1 mark

3 What sort of sandwiches were Mum and Dad making?

Write down **three** sorts.

1...

2...

3... 2 marks

4 What happened to the sandwich on the floor?

Tick one.

The dog ate it. ☐

Dad picked it up. ☐

Sian put it in the bin. ☐

1 mark

Page Total

5 How does Sian describe the noise that came from the car?

.... 1 mark

6 Some bad things happened to Dad.

Number the sentences in the correct order.

The first one has been done for you.

⬜	**He dropped his phone down a rabbit hole.**
⬜	**The car broke down.**
1	**He dropped his sandwich on the floor.**
⬜	**He fell backwards into a marsh.**
⬜	**He couldn't find the picnic spot beside the lake.**

2 marks

7 Write down **three** words to describe how Sian and her family felt as they walked home.

1.

....

2.

....

3.

....

2 marks

End of TEST B

Page Total

HeadStart
primary

Reading Comprehension

YEAR 2

Scaled Score TEST C

Name: ....

Class: ....

Date: ....

Raw Score .... /40

Scaled Score ....

SEEING RAINBOWS

Everyone has seen a rainbow appear in the sky when there is rain and sunshine together. You might also have heard the old tale that, at the end of the rainbow, there is a pot of gold. Of course, no one has ever found it – or ever will.

1 What sort of weather do you need for a rainbow to appear in the sky?

....

1 mark

2 What are you supposed to find at the end of the rainbow? **Tick one**.

sunshine ☐

an old tale ☐

a pot of gold ☐

1 mark

3 Does the writer think anyone will ever find gold at the end of the rainbow? **Circle one**.

Yes   No   Maybe

1 mark

1

Page Total

As you know, a rainbow is a curved shape in the sky. Did you know the different colours are made by the sun's rays being bent as they pass through raindrops? You can't run over to it and touch it, because it isn't solid like a painting of a rainbow on paper. It's just made of light. You also see them around waterfalls or in the spray you make when you're watering the garden.

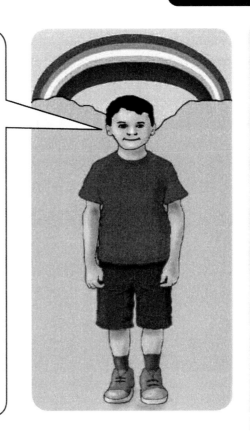

4 Find and copy the word that describes the shape of a rainbow.

....

1 mark

5 What happens to the sun's rays as they pass through a raindrop?

....

1 mark

6 Why can't you touch a rainbow?

....

....

1 mark

Page Total

7 As well as in the sky, you might see a rainbow somewhere else. Find and copy **two** other places where you might see one.

1.
....

2.
....

Page Total

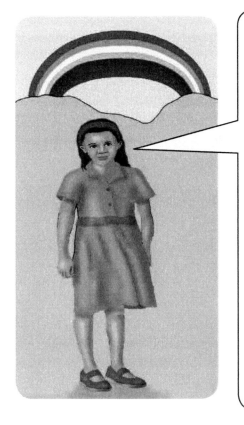

You probably know all the colours in a rainbow: red, orange, yellow, green, blue, indigo and violet. The easiest way to remember the order in which they come is to make up a short sentence. The first letter of each word tells you the colour. This is mine: **R**UN **O**R **Y**OU'LL **G**ET **B**LASTED **I**NTO **V**EG! You can think of a better one. It's amazing that you get all those colours when white light is split up as it passes through drops of water.

8) What colour is the light to begin with, before it is split up into different colours?

....

1 mark

9) The colours of the rainbow are in a certain order.
Write **true** or **false** after these sentences.

Orange comes after red. ....

Blue comes before green. ....

Violet comes after indigo. ....

2 marks

4

Page Total

THE EMPEROR WHO HATED YELLOW
PART 1

The Emperor stood in front of his mirror admiring his beard – the longest beard in the world, he thought. His beloved yellow cat, Mustard, peered in the mirror too, purring. She hardly ever left his side.

Then, one sad day, Mustard vanished. The Emperor commanded his servants to find her. They searched high and low, inside cupboards, behind the curtains and even under the carpets. But Mustard could not be found.

1 Where was the Emperor standing while he was admiring his beard?

....

1 mark

2 Why did the Emperor admire his beard?

....

....

1 mark

5

Page Total

3 What was the name of the Emperor's cat?

....

1 mark

4 **Circle the word** that means the same as **disappeared**.

vanished   peered   beloved

1 mark

5 Name the **three** places that the servants searched.

1.
....

2.
....

3.
....

2 marks

Page Total

When he heard this terrible news, the Emperor told everyone that he hated yellow. The colour reminded him too much of his cat. He refused to eat scrambled eggs, cheese or custard; or drink lemon or pineapple juice. When one of his servants brought him some bananas, he got into a rage.

"Take those horrible yellow things away," he roared, "and paint them purple with orange spots!"

So it went on. If someone served him tea in a yellow cup, he threw it out of the window. If he received yellow socks or a matching yellow hat and scarf for his birthday, they went straight into the bin.

At bedtime, his servants brought him his white teddy bear, his blue cuddly blanket and his red hot water bottle. Even so, he found it hard to sleep and, when he did, all he dreamt about was his yellow cat, Mustard.

6   Why did the Emperor hate anything that was yellow?

....

....   2 marks

7   Find and write down **three** yellow things that the Emperor refused to eat or drink.

1. ....

2. ....

3. ....   2 marks

7

Page Total

8 Find and write down a word that means:
shouted very loudly.

....

1 mark

9 He told his servants to paint the bananas.
What colour?

....

1 mark

10 What did the Emperor do if someone gave him a
yellow hat or scarf?

....

1 mark

11 Why do you think the servants brought him a white
teddy bear at bedtime?

....

....

2 marks

12 What did the Emperor dream about?
Circle one.

bananas   his teddy bear   his cat

1 mark

Page Total

13 If you gave the Emperor a box of coloured pencils, what do you think he would do?

....

....

....

2 marks

Page Total

THE EMPEROR WHO HATED YELLOW
—————— PART 2 ——————

The Emperor was so bad-tempered he moaned that the sun was too yellow. He trudged round his garden on cloudy days. Daffodils grew in secret corners. Yellow canaries sang softly from leafy, dark trees.

One morning, the Emperor grumbled as he combed his long beard. The door opened and in walked his youngest grandchild, Amber. She was dressed from head to toe in yellow, she had golden hair and she was pulling a yellow wooden duck on wheels.

1 Why did the Emperor go outside only when it was cloudy?

.... 1 mark

2 What sort of birds sang in the leafy, dark trees?

.... 1 mark

3 When the Emperor was combing his beard, how do you know he was in a bad mood?

.... 1 mark

4 Who is **Amber**?

....

1 mark

5 Name **three** things about Amber that are yellow.

1. ....

2. ....

3. ....

2 marks

Page Total

"I can't stand yellow!" screeched the Emperor. He snorted and hopped around like a mad chicken on a hot afternoon. He chased Amber round the room, along palace corridors, round corners and up winding stairs. Amber just giggled. When they reached the highest tower of the palace, Amber hid outside on a high balcony.

Hearing the squeak of the duck's wheels, the Emperor rushed out onto the balcony. He tripped over his long beard. Then over the edge he stumbled and tumbled.

He was sure to land with an enormous bump, when up flew a hundred yellow canaries. They caught hold of his beard and, flapping their tiny wings, gently lowered him to the ground.

They laid him in a bed of bright, yellow daffodils and, there, among the flowers, was Mustard, the yellowest cat you have ever seen.

6   The Emperor screeched, **"I can't stand yellow!"** What did he do after that? **Number** the sentences in the correct order. The first one has been done for you.

☐	**He chased Amber round corners.**
1	**He hopped around.**
☐	**He chased Amber up the winding stairs.**
☐	**He chased Amber round the room.**
☐	**He chased Amber along corridors.**

2 marks

Page Total

7 Where did Amber hide?

....

1 mark

8 How did the Emperor know where Amber was hiding?

....

....

1 mark

9 How did the yellow canaries save the Emperor?

....

....

1 mark

End of TEST C

Page Total

HeadStart
primary

YEAR 2

Reading Comprehension

ANSWERS & MARK SCHEME

Scaled Score TESTS A, B & C

Once a test has been marked, a raw score out of 40 can be awarded.
This score should then be converted to a scaled score using the conversion charts in the digital version.

The table below can then be used to identify progress against one of the 6 stages. (See notes in the digital version for further information.)

Year 2

NB: The stage boundaries and 3 'standards' in the table below are intended as a guide to children's progress. They should not be interpreted in the same way as a scaled score of 100 is used as 'standard met' in KS1 and KS2 SATs.

Scaled Score	Stage	
0 - 75	Emerging	Working towards the expected standard
76 - 95	Developing	
96 - 100	Progressing	Working within the expected standard
101 - 112	Secure	
113 - 122	Exceeding	Working above the expected standard
123 +	Exceeding with greater depth	

The assessments are intended to be used by teachers as a tool to support their professional judgement. The table above should be used only as a guide to achievement and progress. This data should always be used in conjunction with ongoing teacher assessment.

1

Content domain

The text and table below are taken directly from the 'Key Stage 1 English reading test framework'. This document is used by test designers to create the Key Stage 1 SAT.

The appropriate 'domains' are identified in the following HeadStart mark scheme.

4. Content domain

The content domain sets out the relevant elements from the national curriculum programme of study (2014) for English at key stage 1 that are assessed in the English reading test. The tests will, over time, sample from each area of the content domain.

The key stage 1 English reading tests will focus on the comprehension elements of the national curriculum.

Table 2 shows the content domain, which sets out how elements of the curriculum will be defined for test development purposes.

Table 2: Content domain relating to questions

	Content domain reference
1a	draw on knowledge of vocabulary to understand texts
1b	identify / explain key aspects of fiction and non-fiction texts, such as characters, events, titles and information
1c	identify and explain the sequence of events in texts
1d	make inferences from the text
1e	predict what might happen on the basis of what has been read so far

2

Can't Do Anything

No.	Answers and Mark Scheme	Domain	Marks
1	She's too little.	1b	1
2	She offers him her doll to take to school.	1d	1
3	he's annoyed	1d	1
4	Mo and Jo ------------------ end of the lane Connie --------------------- bridge over the river Alex ------------------------ winding road **[All three answers have to be correct for 2 marks.]**	1b	2
5	Mo and Jo	1b	1
6	twigs and leaves	1b	1
7	Connie	1b	1
8	sad	1a	1
9	Everyone cheers.	1d	1
10	hammer	1b	1
11	Mo and Jo ----------------------- car Connie ------------------------- dolphin Alex ------------------------------ mobile **[All three answers have to be correct for 2 marks.]**	1b	2
12	**1**. bridge **2**. rocks **3**. trees **4**. winding road **[Award 2 marks for putting the remaining three in the correct order.]**	1c	2
13	She says, "Can I have this toy?"/She thinks it looks like a toy.	1b	1
14	lump and block **[Accept 'chunk' from earlier section of the story.]**	1a	1
15	1 mark for a literal description of what happened at home, e.g. Tara thought it looked like a hippo/his mother thought he was clever. Another mark for how he cheered up/felt differently about his block of wood. **OR:** 2 marks for an answer based on inference, e.g. comments designed to save face in front of his friends: what a great toy he made/how he thought his sister would like it/can't wait to make another one, etc.	1e	2

The Rubbish Band

No.	Answers and Mark Scheme	Domain	Marks
1	They beat them to tell farmers to come for dinner.	1b	1
2	loud	1a	1
3	Mum gave her an old baking tray. = 1 mark Dad drilled holes in the top. = 1 mark	1b	2
4	She wanted to decorate it / to make it look colourful / nice.	1d	1
5	Takisha's beater is a wooden spoon [= 1 mark] and her mother might need it in the kitchen / to cook / bake. [= 1 mark]	1d	2
6	They asked the spirits to make it rain.	1b	1
7	cactus	1b	1
8	**1**. found a cardboard tube **2**. taped brown paper over one end **3**. put in twisted tin foil **4**. put in rice and dried pasta **5**. taped paper over the other end **6**. decorated it **[All must be in the correct order for 2 marks.]**	1c	2
9	It sounds like rain when you turn it upside down. [= 1 mark] The stuff inside (rice, pasta) trickles down. [= 1 mark]	1b	2
10	xylophone	1d	1
11	saw = 1 mark scissors = 1 mark	1b	2
12	Grandad	1b	1
13	Different sized pipes make different notes (when struck).	1d	1
14	Takisha	1b	1
15	The children recycled rubbish when making their instruments. [= 1 mark] The band's not very good yet. / They need more practice. Quoting Tom: "We are rubbish." [= 1 mark]	1d	2

	TOTAL	40

4

The slow-worm

No.	Answers and Mark Scheme	Domain	Marks
1	It's not a worm. = 1 mark It's not slow. = 1 mark	1b	2
2	It has no legs. It can blink.	1b	1
3	false - true - true - false **[Award 2 marks for four correct answers; 1 mark for three correct answers.]**	1b	2
4	between 30cm and 40cm	1b	1
5	(rough) grassland, (edge of) woodland, garden / compost heap **[Award 2 marks for three correct answers; 1 mark for two correct answers.]**	1b	2
6	slugs / snails / (some) insects	1b	1
7	Spring is when they come out of hibernation. / They bask in the sunshine to warm up their bodies.	1b	1
8	A slow-worm will not hurt you.	1a	1

5

The Night Patrol

No.	Answers and Mark Scheme	Domain	Marks
1	Any three of: buzz / whistle / hoot / screech / whine / bark	1a	1
2	vole / mole [Accept 'control' from verse 4.]	1b	1
3	wide-eyed	1a	1
4	fox	1b	1
5	1. vole 2. owl 3. badger 4. fox **[All four must be in the correct order for 2 marks.]**	1c	2
6	swoop, leap	1a	1
7	vole / mole / rabbit / mouse / moth **[Award 2 marks for three correct answers; 1 mark for two correct answers.]**	1b	2

Nocturnal Animals

No.	Answers and Mark Scheme	Domain	Marks
1	200	1b	1
2	500	1b	1
3	fox	1b	1
4	They are sharp for digging.	1b	1
5	claws	1a	1
6	badger / owl / fox **[Award 2 marks for three correct answers; 1 mark for two correct answers.]**	1b	2
7	frogs	1b	1
8	owl	1b	1
9	badger -------------------------- underground bat --------------------------------- barn hedgehog ----------------------- hedgerow	1b	1

A Lovely Day for a Picnic

No.	Answers and Mark Scheme	Domain	Marks
1	Not a cloud in the sky.	1b	1
2	six o'clock in the morning	1b	1
3	tuna, egg, cheese **[Award 2 marks for three correct answers; 1 mark for two correct answers.]**	1b	2
4	The dog (Charlie) ate it.	1b/1d	1
5	strange clonking noise	1b	1
6	1. He dropped his sandwich on the floor. 2. The car broke down. 3. He couldn't find the picnic spot beside the lake. 4. He dropped his phone down a rabbit hole. 5. He fell backwards into a marsh. **[All four remaining sentences must be in the correct order for 2 marks.]**	1c	2
7	tired, disappointed, hungry [Accept 'sunburnt'.] **[Award 2 marks for three correct answers; 1 mark for two correct answers.]**	1b	2
		TOTAL	40

8

Seeing Rainbows

No.	Answers and Mark Scheme	Domain	Marks
1	rain and sunshine (together)	1b	1
2	a pot of gold	1b	1
3	No	1d	1
4	curved	1a	1
5	They are bent.	1b	1
6	It isn't solid. / It's just made of light.	1b	1
7	around waterfalls = 1 mark in the garden / in the spray when you're watering the garden = 1 mark	1b	2
8	white	1b	1
9	Orange comes after red ------------------------- true Blue comes before green ----------------------- false Violet comes after indigo ----------------------- true **[Award 2 marks for three correct answers; 1 mark for two correct answers.]**	1b	2

9

The Emperor Who Hated Yellow (part 1)

No.	Answers and Mark Scheme	Domain	Marks
1	in front of his mirror	1b	1
2	It was the longest beard in the world.	1d	1
3	Mustard	1b	1
4	vanished	1a	1
5	inside cupboards / behind the curtains / under the carpets **[Award 2 marks for all three correct answers; 1 mark for two correct answers.]**	1b	2
6	Anything that was yellow made him think of his cat, Mustard. [= 1 mark] Thinking of his cat made him sad. [= 1 mark]	1d	2
7	scrambled eggs / cheese / lemon juice / pineapple juice / custard / bananas **[Award 2 marks for all three correct answers; 1 mark for two correct answers.]**	1b	2
8	roared	1a	1
9	purple with orange spots	1b	1
10	It went straight into the bin.	1b	1
11	They didn't want to bring him a yellow teddy bear [= 1 mark] in case it upset him. [= 1 mark]	1d	2
12	his cat	1b	1
13	He might get angry when he sees yellow pencils inside. = [1 mark] **OR** He might throw away the yellow pencils [= 1 mark] and keep the others. [= 1 mark] **OR** He might use the yellow pencils [= 1 mark] to draw pictures of his cat. [= 1 mark]	1e	2

10

The Emperor Who Hated Yellow (part 2)

No.	Answers and Mark Scheme	Domain	Marks
1	The sun was too yellow. / The clouds covered the yellow sun.	1b	1
2	yellow canaries	1b	1
3	He grumbled.	1d	1
4	his youngest grandchild	1b	1
5	dressed in yellow (from head to toe) / yellow wooden duck / golden hair / her name was Amber **[Award 2 marks for three correct answers; 1 mark for two correct answers.]**	1b	2
6	1. He hopped around. 2. He chased Amber round the room. 3. He chased Amber along corridors. 4. He chased Amber round corners. 5. He chased Amber up the winding stairs.	1c	2
7	outside on a high balcony	1b	1
8	He could hear the wooden duck's wheels squeaking.	1b	1
9	They flew up, caught hold of his beard and lowered him safely to the ground.	1b	1

	TOTAL	40

PLEASE NOTE:

The CD-ROM/digital version also contains the book and tests filed separately for printing. A full answer version and colour digital versions of the book and tests are also included.

The raw score/scaled score conversion charts are also supplied.

PLEASE NOTE:

The digital version also contains the book and tests filed separately for printing. A full answer version and colour digital versions of the book and tests are also included.

The raw score/scaled score conversion charts are also supplied.